About

SHAKESPEARE

William Shakespeare, regarded as the greatest writer in the English language, was born in Stratford-upon-Avon in Warwickshire, England (around April 23, 1564). He was the third of eight children born to John and Mary Shakespeare.

Shakespeare was a poet, playwright, and dramatist. He is often known as England's national poet and the "Bard of Avon." Thirty-eight plays, 154 sonnets, two long narrative poems, and several other poems are attributed to him. Shakespeare's plays have been translated into every major language and are performed more often than those of any other playwright.

MAIN CHARACTERS

Helena is the daughter of the finest doctor in France. Her father died leaving her ward to the Countess of Rousillon. She loves Bertram, the countess's son.

Bertram is a handsome young man and a skilled soldier. He is the countess's son. He unwillingly marries Helena before abandoning her.

The Widow of Florence is a kindly woman who takes in Helena when she arrives in Florence. She and her daughter, Diana, help Helena get her husband back.

The King of France likes Helena and is upset about Bertram's behavior toward her.

Diana is an honorable maiden who Bertram falls in love with. She and her mother, the Widow of Florence, help Helena get her husband back.

ALL'S WELL THAT ENDS WELL

The handsome soldier Bertram had been named the Count of Rousillon a short while ago after his father died, leaving him the title and the

estate. The King of France and Bertram's father were very close friends, so the moment the king learned of his friend's death, he sent for Bertram to offer him his special favor and to bring him under his protection.

Lafeu, an old minister in the French court, came to inform Bertram of the king's intentions. Since the king was the absolute monarch in France at that time, any order he gave had to be obeyed. Bertram knew that he

would have to go back with Lafeu immediately. His mother was sad to see her son go away so soon after she had lost her husband. But Lafeu reassured her that the king was very kind and wanted to take young Bertram under his wing after the death of his father. He also told her that the king was suffering from a very serious malady for which there seemed to be no cure. At this, Bertram's mother mentioned Helena, a young girl who lived with her, and her late father. She explained that Helena's father, Gerard de Narbon, had been a great physician, able to cure almost any disease. At the time of his death, he had wished

11

that his only daughter, Helena, should come to stay with Bertram's mother, and Helena had lived with her ever since. She also told him how Helena had inherited all her father's virtues and his excellent disposition.

While Bertram's mother spoke of the great Gerard

de Narbon, Helena, who was close by, started weeping.

Soon, Bertram bade his mother goodbye. The Countess asked Lafeu to take good care of her son, for he was still an unseasoned courtier. Before leaving, Bertram spoke to Helena, asking her to take good care of his mother.

While it was true that Helena had been very fond of her late father, her tears were for another reason entirely. She had long been in love with Bertram, and now that he was going away, she could no longer conceal her sadness. But she also knew how different they both were. While Bertram was the Count of Rousillon, Helena was just the daughter of a humble physician. Therefore, she considered herself lucky to be the servant of the house and looked upon Bertram as her master.

Helena's father had left her some prescriptions of rare virtue, which he had acquired through his long study and experience in medicine. As she went through them once again, she found an antidote for the illness the king had contracted.

Helena made a secret pact with herself that she would go to Paris and cure the king of his disease. But then more pragmatic thoughts crossed her mind; after all, had the king's own physicians not told him that his illness was incurable? Why, then,

would he listen to the advice
of a young girl? But she knew
that her father's revered cures
were perhaps her only chance
to one day become the wife of
Bertram, the Count of Rousillon.

While Helena was
pondering the matter and

speaking her thoughts out loud,
a steward who worked with her
overheard what she said. He
immediately went to Bertram's
mother and told her what he
had heard. But instead of being
angry with Helena, Bertram's
mother just smiled, remembering
her own youthful days. "Love

20

is a thorn that belongs to the rose of youth," she said.

Helena entered the room, unaware that the lady of the house knew all about her feelings. Bertram's mother spoke to her very kindly and told her how she felt like a mother to her, but Helena just turned pale at the words and realized her love for Bertram was no longer a secret. She expressed how fortunate she was to have such a kind

mistress, but Bertram's mother kept declaring her motherly feelings toward Helena. Finally, the young girl blurted out, "Pardon me, madam, but you

are not my mother; the Count of Rousillon cannot be my brother, nor I your daughter."

Only then did the noble Count-mother say, "But you can

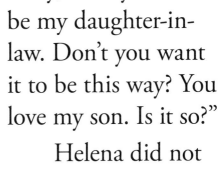

be my daughter-in-law. Don't you want it to be this way? You love my son. Is it so?"

Helena did not know what to say. When she finally confessed, Bertram's mother asked her if she wanted to go to Paris to be with Bertram. Helena merely replied that it was not just

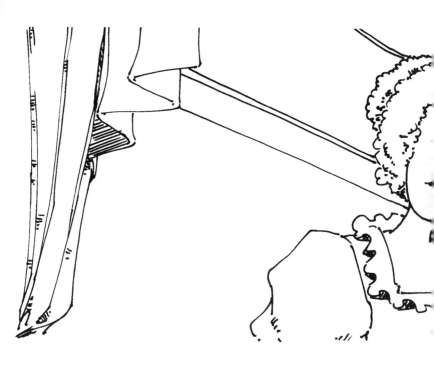

Bertram she had been thinking of in connection with her visit to Paris. She mentioned the king's illness and how she knew of a remedy that had belonged to her father, which would surely cure the ailing monarch. The Count-mother knew that this would perhaps be the finest moment for Gerard de Narbon's

daughter to announce herself to the world, so she immediately gave her leave to head for Paris, along with enough money and attendants to accompany her.

Once she reached Paris, Helena got in touch with the kind old Lafeu and told him of the remedy  that would surely cure the king. However, it was not easy for her to be seen by the monarch. After all, why would the king trust a young girl's medicines, when all the physicians in the country had failed? But Helena informed him that she was indeed the daughter of the great Gerard de Narbon, someone the king had always held in high regard, so the king decided to go ahead with the treatment. But before Helena could administer the medicine, the king made

a deal with her—if the medicine did not cure him in two days' time, then Helena would pay for it with her life; however, if he were to recover, then she had the right to choose a husband from

all the men present in the whole of France.

Helena had indeed been right about her father's medicinal powers, for before the two days had passed, the king was well again. He claimed that he had never felt as healthy as he did now. He agreed that he had lost the wager with Helena and asked all the noblemen in his court to assemble before them. Helena went round and finally spotted Bertram. She informed the king of her

choice and the king was only too happy with it. But Bertram was not amused and showed clear disdain toward the proceedings, refusing to marry the daughter of a poor physician and someone who worked in his own house.

The king was livid with Bertram's behavior. Helena's choice had been the result of a royal wager, and Bertram was clearly being disrespectful toward him. So, though Helena said Bertram did not have

to marry her, the king ordered the marriage to take place. And so, very soon, Bertram and Helena were married. But it was a sad marriage, since Bertram did not love Helena at all.

As soon as the marriage was

concluded, Bertram
asked the king for
leave of absence. Before
leaving, Bertram told
Helena to go back to
his mother and take
good care of her. He
informed her that this
sudden marriage had
shaken him considerably
and he wanted to be by
himself. Helena only
replied that, as his most
obedient servant, she
would continue to do as
he wished, but Bertram
was already gone.

Helena went back to
the Count-mother with

a heavy heart. She had met both her objectives in traveling to France—curing the king's disease and also marrying the man of her dreams—yet she had brought back with her no joy. What hurt her the most was the letter she received from Bertram when she reached Rousillon, telling her that only if she could remove the ring from his finger, which he would never remove on his own, could she call him her husband.

The Count-mother tried her best to console

her, but Helena's broken heart
could find no solace in her
arms. She kept staring at a
particular phrase in the letter,
which said, "Till I have no
wife, I have nothing in France."
Neither Helena nor her mother-
in-law could believe the cruel

words that Bertram had written in the letter to his wife.

The next morning, when the Count-mother awoke, Helena was nowhere to be found. Finally, one of the servants brought her a letter from Helena, which said that the poor girl was so heartbroken by Bertram's

actions that she had decided
to leave Rousillon and go on a
pilgrimage to the shrine of St.
Jacques le Grand. She begged her
mother-in-law's forgiveness and

asked her to inform her son that the wife he so detested had gone away, so he could return home.

Meanwhile, Bertram had left France for the Italian city of Florence, where he had become an officer in the duke's army. After fighting many valiant wars, he had distinguished himself through his brave actions.

One day, Bertram received a letter from his mother informing him that his wife had left forever, so he decided to return home. Little did he know that destiny had recently brought a young pilgrim to Florence, none other than Helena.

The shrine of St. Jacques le Grand, the place to which Helena was going, was a short distance from Florence. Once Helena reached the beautiful city, she decided to go to a kind widow who offered lodgings to female pilgrims and looked after them during their

stay in Florence. The widow very kindly welcomed Helena and offered to show her the sights around the city. She mentioned that she would also take her to see the duke's army, and she could perhaps even meet a fellow

countryman serving in the
army, the Count of Rousillon.

Helena did not need
to be asked twice and got
ready to visit the army
immediately. When they saw
Bertram from a distance, the

widow casually remarked, "Is he not handsome?"

Helena simply said in return, "I like him well."

The lady then went on to tell Helena about Bertram's past, and how he had run away to Florence to escape from his wife. As the lady continued her story, Helena's heart sank. The widow told her about Bertram's

love for a woman called Diana, her own daughter. He would try to meet her after the rest of the family had retired for the night, singing love songs in praise of her beauty. But Diana knew that Bertram was a married man and therefore did not reciprocate his feelings of love. Helena also learned

from her hostess that Bertram
was going to leave Florence
forever the next morning.

Helena immediately came
up with a plan to reclaim her
truant husband. She made

confessed to the widow that she was the wife of the Count, and the old widow at once agreed to help her in any way possible to make Bertram fall in love with her. So Diana, her daughter, sent

a message to Bertram saying that she would like to see him one last time before he left for France.

To make sure Bertram wouldn't suspect anything, Helena had another message sent to him stating that she had died during the pilgrimage.

When Bertram stole into
Diana's chambers that night,
he found the woman of his
dreams waiting for him. Little
did he know that the woman
in the room was not Diana, but
Helena. Unable to tell them apart
in the dark, Bertram promised

to marry Diana and said
he would love her forever.

Helena started
speaking to him about love
and how she too wanted
to marry him. It was a pity
that he would be leaving
tomorrow, as she was sure
he would forget about her
in France. But Bertram,
hearing Diana reciprocate
his feelings for the first
time, promised that he
would be back to ask for
her hand in marriage.
Now was the golden
opportunity that Helena
had been waiting for, and
she asked Bertram to give

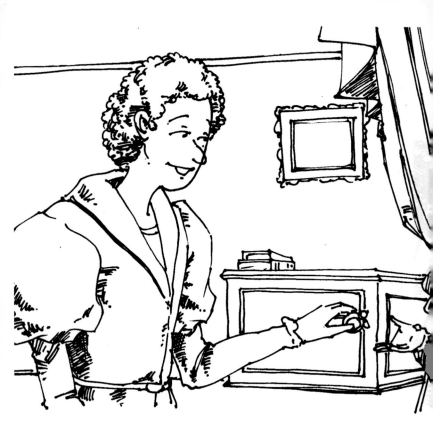

her his ring to remind her of
him, saying he would surely
come back to reclaim it. Perhaps
then, they could get married.

Bertram was so excited by
the proposal that he handed
Helena the ring, still thinking

she was Diana. Helena in turn handed him her own ring, which in the darkness of the night Bertram did not recognize. Before morning, Helena sent Bertram away. Then, along with Diana and her mother, she set off for Paris. There she learned that the king had gone to visit her mother-in-law at her house in Rousillon. So Helena, with her entourage, made for Rousillon, close on the king's heels.

Meanwhile, the king had reached Rousillon and was talking tenderly to Bertram's mother about the late Helena, the girl who had cured him and whom her foolish son had rejected. Lafeu started weeping, remembering the sweet girl he had helped seek an audience with the king. Just then, Bertram entered the room, and the king noticed Helena's ring on his finger. This aroused his suspicions, as he remembered that Bertram had not been wearing it when he left France. He wondered if he had met Helena later and killed her, thereby acquiring the ring.

Diana and her mother entered the hall and entreated the king to marry Bertram to Diana, the girl he had promised

to marry while in Florence.
Diana went on to present the ring
Bertram had given her during
his last night in the Italian city.

Bertram, scared that the
king would severely punish

him, immediately started to deny the whole affair. But the king was livid and ordered his guards to arrest both Bertram and Diana, and hold them until they told him the truth.

At that very moment, Helena entered and revealed herself to the people present. Bertram's mother, the king, and Lafeu were overjoyed to see her alive and well. She explained how the rings had been exchanged, and everything

that had happened between them in Florence. She then turned to Bertram and showed him the letter, which said that only if she could remove the ring from his finger could she call him her husband.

Bertram was surprised and touched by the love Helena felt for him. He promised he would love her dearly and forever.

The king, pleased to hear of Diana's part in helping Helena find happiness, promised Diana that he would find

her a noble husband as well.
Bertram and Helena were now
in love and ready to live the
rest of their lives together.

As most often is the case,
all's well that ends well.